Becoming an E.I. Guy:

The 28-Day Beginner's Guide to Emotional Intelligence for the Modern Man

Evan Hunter Jr., LPC, LADC

Forward Progress Counseling, LLC

Waterbury, CT

© 2024 Evan Hunter Jr., LPC, LADC. All rights reserved.

Published by Forward Progress Counseling LLC.

No part of this publication may be reproduced, distributed, or transmitted in any form or by any means, including photocopying, recording, or other electronic or mechanical methods, without the prior written permission of the publisher, except in the case of brief quotations embodied in critical reviews and certain other noncommercial uses permitted by copyright law. For permission requests, write to the publisher, addressed "Attention: Permissions Coordinator," at ejhunter@forwardprogresscounseling.org.

Table of Contents

Dedication......

Acknowledgements......

Who This Book Is For......

Introduction......

Chapter 1: Understanding Emotional Intelligence......page 1

Chapter 2: Self-Awareness......page 7

Chapter 3: Self-Management......page 14

Chapter 4: Social Awareness......page 19

Chapter 5: Relationship Management......page 25

Chapter 6: Emotional Intelligence in Relationships......page 31

Chapter 7: Emotional Intelligence at Work......page 37

Chapter 8: Emotional Intelligence as a Dad......page 43

Conclusion: Transformational Power of EI......page 49

How To Use This Workbook......page 54

Dedication

This book is dedicated to my city, Waterbury, CT. This little boy from the Southside would not be the man I am today if it wasn't for my hometown – the good, the bad, and the ugly. I love you all, and I hope this book can save a life.

Emotional Intelligence courses and Socioemotional Learning classes are something we need in all our schools and curriculums! If we learned it at an earlier age, imagine where we'd be now? With that said, it's NEVER TOO LATE!

To Andrea, Ella, and Emery. My heartbeats! Your unconditional love and support in everything I do cannot be overlooked. You all mean the world to me. To my parents, and siblings; I love you all so much and I hope you can take something out of this book to apply to your own journeys. And yall know I am here every step of the way!

To the Team…I wrote this book with you fellas in mind. Let's keep progressing! Yall already know #TG

Acknowledgements

First, I'd like to thank God of course because without Him, none of this would be possible. I am a humble servant. I can remember being told there was a calling on my life, to change lives, and I believe that I am walking that path right now.

I am also grateful for my daddy, Evan Hunter Sr., for reviewing this book for me and providing the wise insight that he has always provided to me my entire life. I am forever grateful for you, Pops!

And last, but not least, I want to thank you, the reader. For taking this time out for YOU to embark on this journey of enhancing your emotional intelligence.

This is something that we've long overlooked, fellas. But now is the time to get our minds and emotions right!

Who This Book Is For

I'd like to start by stating that this book is not for everybody; and that is alright! Although the title is geared specifically for men, I'd like to highlight that the ideas and strategies shared in this book can transcend gender and be helpful in many different everyday life situations. Ladies, if you are reading this, I am glad you are here, also! Just please keep in mind, that this book is designed for the fellas, so all of the language will be in the framework of speaking to the guys. But, I think anybody can benefit from this book.

If you are a person seeking to improve interpersonal skills at work and in personal relationships while hoping to communicate more effectively; if you are a parent striving to better understand and connect with your children through improved emotional awareness and communication; or if you are someone facing challenges in managing your stress and emotions in high-pressure environments for various reasons, then this book is for you! If you are a leader looking to facilitate a more emotionally intelligent workplace and be promote a supportive team dynamic, or simply a person interested in personal growth and understanding of emotional intelligence on happiness and overall success, I hope you find it here! At the end of the book is a workbook to follow along with throughout the 28-day experience. #GODSPEED! Go Out and Deliver Some Positive Energy, Every Day!

Introduction

Imagine standing at the free-throw line, the game clock ticking down its final seconds. Your team is one point behind. The weight of the moment rests on your shoulders. You've practiced for this, mentally and physically, but what truly sets you apart in this moment isn't just your skill with the ball—it's your emotional intelligence (EI). It's the deep breath you take to calm your nerves, the way you tune out the crowd's roar, focusing solely on the hoop in front of you. This is the power of emotional intelligence: the ability to manage your emotions and the emotions of others, to turn a pressure-cooked situation into a triumphant win.

Welcome to The Emotionally Intelligent Man, and I am glad you are here. This journey isn't about changing who you are but unlocking the full potential of your emotional capabilities to improve every facet of your life. As a licensed counselor, husband, father, brother, son, uncle, friend, etc., I've seen firsthand how developing emotional intelligence can transform relationships, enhance career success, and lead to a more fulfilled life.

Over the next four weeks and beyond, you'll embark on a transformative journey. Like mastering any new skill, it'll require practice, patience, and a bit of strategy—think of it as learning to play chess, where anticipating your opponent's moves and understanding the board's dynamics lead to victory. Only in this game, the board is your life, and the moves are your emotions.

In this book, you will gain an understanding of Emotional Intelligence as a whole, its importance, and some real-life stories and examples of how to apply and enhance it in your everyday life. In this book, you will gain an understanding of Emotional Intelligence as a whole, its importance, and some real- life stories and examples of how to apply and enhance it in your everyday life. At the end of the book is a workbook to follow along with the book during the next month, as well. Buckle up, boys! We're going on a ride!

Chapter 1 – Understanding Emotional Intelligence

The Essence of Emotional Intelligence

Emotional intelligence, at its core, is like possessing an internal compass that guides your interactions with yourself and the world around you. It's about having the self-awareness to recognize your emotions as they surface, understanding why they've appeared, and knowing how to express them appropriately (Mayer, J. D., & Salovey, P.,1997). But it doesn't stop with self-awareness; emotional intelligence also involves being attuned to the emotions of others, interpreting them accurately, and responding with empathy and understanding.

Daniel Goleman, a pioneer in the study of emotional intelligence, emphasizes its critical role in our lives. According to

Goleman, emotional intelligence is the bedrock of meaningful relationships, professional success, and personal satisfaction. It's not merely an asset but a fundamental component of human interaction. In his seminal book, "Emotional Intelligence" (1995), Goleman posits that emotional intelligence is as crucial, if not more so, than IQ in determining success in life and work. He identifies five key elements of emotional intelligence: self-awareness, self-regulation, internal motivation, empathy, and social skills. He broke them down more simply into four quadrants, which we will explore below. These elements serve as the framework for developing and applying emotional intelligence in various aspects of life.

Imagine navigating life's challenges with the precision and grace of a seasoned athlete. Just as an athlete uses strength, strategy, and skill to overcome obstacles and achieve their goals, emotional intelligence enables you to manage your emotions, forge strong relationships, and achieve your personal and professional objectives. It's about more than just controlling your temper or managing stress; it's about understanding the nuances of human emotion and using that understanding to navigate the complexities of interpersonal relationships and personal growth.

Goleman's research underscores the transformative power of emotional intelligence, demonstrating its profound impact on everything from leadership effectiveness to personal well-being. By developing emotional intelligence, you're not just learning to manage your emotions; you're unlocking the door to a more fulfilling, balanced, and successful life.

The Four Quadrants of Emotional Intelligence

Self-Awareness: Like a quarterback reading the defense, self-awareness is about understanding your emotions, strengths, and weaknesses.

Self-Management: This is your ability to adapt to changing circumstances—calling an audible when the original play isn't going to work.

Social Awareness: Imagine being a coach who can read the mood of his team and the opposing team, understanding others' emotions and needs.

Relationship Management: This involves the strategies you use to interact positively with others—like a point guard who knows just when to pass the ball for an assist.

A Tale of Two Players

Let me share a story from my own life. As a father of two daughters, I've had to learn

Becoming an E.I. Guy

the delicate art of managing not just my emotions but also being in tune with theirs. One evening, Ella, my 6-year-old Kindergartener who is learning how to read (and doing very well at it, might I add #ProudDad), was struggling with her homework, frustration written all over her face. My initial instinct was to offer solutions, but recalling the principles of emotional intelligence, I realized she needed empathy, not answers.

We talked about times when I faced similar challenges, sharing a laugh over my own challenges at work earlier that day or even a moment where I struggled to learn something new. This moment of vulnerability opened a dialogue, easing her stress and making the problem-solving process a team effort. It was a small, personal victory, but it underscored the power of emotional intelligence in strengthening relationships.

As a reflection of this chapter, I want you to think of a recent moment when you experienced strong emotions. How did you react? Could understanding your emotional response better have changed the outcome?

Conclusion

As we wrap up this section, remember that developing emotional intelligence is like honing your skills in a sport. It takes time, practice, and sometimes, a coach's guidance. I'm here to guide you through this process, sharing both professional insights and personal anecdotes to light the way.

In the next sections, we'll take a closer look into each quadrant, exploring how to apply these concepts to enhance your relationships, work life, and parenting skills. Stay tuned for a journey that promises to redefine what it means to be an emotionally intelligent man.

Chapter 2 – The Quadrant of Self-Awareness

The Bedrock of Emotional Intelligence

Self-Awareness is the cornerstone upon which the mansion of emotional intelligence is built. It's akin to knowing every nook and cranny of your home, understanding how each part contributes to its warmth and stability. In the realm of emotional intelligence, self-awareness is about recognizing your emotional state, understanding your strengths and weaknesses, and realizing how your emotions affect your thoughts and actions.

The Importance of Self-Awareness

Imagine you're a seasoned basketball player; you know your hot spots on the court, understand when you're likely to miss a shot, and recognize the signs of fatigue setting in. This level of self-knowledge allows you to make real-time adjustments, whether it's passing the ball, taking a moment to catch your breath, or changing your defensive stance. Similarly, emotional self-awareness enables you to navigate life's challenges and opportunities with greater ease and confidence. It allows you to:

Understand and manage your reactions: Knowing your emotional triggers can help you prepare for and manage your reactions to various situations, reducing stress and improving decision-making.

Enhance your relationships: By understanding your emotions, you can communicate more effectively, avoid misunderstandings, and build stronger, more empathetic connections with others.

Promote personal growth: Self-awareness lays the foundation for personal development, helping you to identify areas for improvement and celebrate your strengths.

A Story from the Field

Let's draw from a moment in my career as a counselor. I once worked with a client, let's call him John, a dedicated father and a hardworking professional, who struggled with sudden bursts of anger that were affecting his relationships at home and work. Through our sessions, John learned to identify the signs of his mounting frustration early on, understanding that it often stemmed from feeling out of control or unappreciated.

This revelation was his self-awareness breakthrough. By recognizing these emotional cues, John could take steps to manage his anger, such as taking deep breaths, expressing his feelings in a constructive manner, or even stepping away from situations temporarily to cool down. His journey to self-awareness improved his relationships and job satisfaction significantly.

Building Blocks of Self-Awareness

To cultivate self-awareness, consider the following strategies:

Reflect on Your Emotions: Spend time each day reflecting on your emotional experiences. Ask yourself what you felt, why you felt that way, and how your emotions influenced your actions.

Emotion Journal: Start an emotional journal. Each day, write down at least one emotional experience and analyze your response. This will enhance your self-awareness, the first step in mastering emotional intelligence. This can be found at the end of the book.

Mindfulness Practices: Techniques like meditation can help you become more aware of your present emotional state, thoughts, and bodily sensations, enhancing your self-awareness.

Becoming an E.I. Guy

You guys heard of Phil Jackson before, right? They called him the Zen Master for a reason. His ability to get his teams focused on the present moment through mindfulness made him one of the most successful basketball coaches in the history of the sport.

Emotional Self-Awareness Questions

At the end of each day for the next week, take a few moments to answer the following questions in your journal. This exercise is designed to enhance your emotional self-awareness and help you become more attuned to your emotional landscape.

What were the predominant emotions I felt today?

What triggered these emotions?

How did I react to these emotions? Did I manage them effectively?

How did my emotions affect my interactions with others?

What can I learn from today's emotional experiences?

Reflections and Next Steps

As you begin to answer these questions regularly, patterns will emerge, shedding light on your emotional triggers, reactions, and management strategies. This self-knowledge is invaluable, providing a roadmap for personal growth and improved emotional intelligence.

Self-awareness is a journey, not a destination. Like a chess master who continually studies the board to improve their strategy, your quest for self-awareness requires patience, persistence, and curiosity. Remember, the better you know yourself, the more adept you become at navigating life's complexities with grace and resilience.

In the next chapter, we'll explore the second quadrant of emotional intelligence, Self-

Management, and how you can use your self-awareness to effectively regulate your emotions and behaviors.

Chapter 3: The Quadrant of Self-Management

Mastering Your Emotional Landscape

With the foundation of self-awareness laid, we venture into the territory of Self-Management, the ability to take charge of your emotions and apply them towards constructive activities and positive thinking. If self-awareness is about recognizing your emotions, self-management is about deciding what to do with them. Imagine you're a skilled sailor navigating the vast ocean of your emotions. Self-awareness helps you identify the wind's direction and strength, while self-management allows you to adjust the sails accordingly, steering your ship towards your desired destination. It's like Moana and Maui, and that little chicken that was on the boat with them, know what I mean?

Becoming an E.I. Guy

The Significance of Self-Management

Self-Management is crucial for several reasons. It equips you with the ability to remain calm under pressure, maintain a positive attitude in the face of adversity, and act thoughtfully rather than impulsively. In the context of emotional intelligence, self-management is what allows you to:

<u>Stay composed and positive:</u> Even in challenging situations, you can keep your emotions in check, projecting confidence and resilience.

<u>Follow through on commitments</u>: Self-discipline helps you stick to your goals and see tasks through to completion.

<u>Adapt to change</u>: Flexibility enables you to adjust to new circumstances and find solutions in the face of obstacles.

Becoming an E.I. Guy

Lessons from the (football) Field

Reflecting on my experiences, I recall running my own recreational flag football team. One game stands out when we were trailing by a couple of scores during the championship game. Frustration bubbled up among the players, and as the captain, I felt it too. However, I realized that giving in to frustration would only demoralize the team further. I took a deep breath, gathered my thoughts, and focused on what we could control—our effort and attitude. By managing my emotions, I was able to encourage the team, and we slowly chipped away at the lead and eventually winning the game (shout out to the #BoomSquad). This experience underscored the power of self-management in leading by example and uplifting others. Make no mistake, though. I've had moments where I was not as calm and made the situation worse. I hate losing!

Strategies for Enhancing Self-Management

To improve your self-management skills, consider implementing the following practices:

<u>*Set Clear Goals*</u>: Like a quarterback focusing on the next play, set specific, achievable objectives for yourself. This clarity can help direct your emotional energy positively.

<u>*Practice Mindfulness*</u>: This skill is absolutely worth mentioning again. As previously mentioned, mindfulness is an important practice for emotional regulation and management. The more in control of yourself you are, the most in control of the situation you are.

<u>*Develop Coping Strategies*</u>: Identify activities that help you relieve stress, such as exercise, reading, or talking with friends. These can be valuable tools in your emotional self-management toolkit. The more tools you have available, the more equipped you will be when

life decides to start lifing out of nowhere, per usual.

Moving Forward

As you practice these exercises and integrate self-management strategies into your life, you'll find yourself better equipped to navigate emotional challenges with grace and effectiveness. Remember, self-management is about making conscious choices in response to your emotions, steering your life in the direction you choose.

In the next chapter, we'll explore the third quadrant of emotional intelligence, Social Awareness, and how enhancing your understanding of others' emotions can enrich your relationships and interactions.

Chapter 4: The Quadrant of Social Awareness

Navigating the Social Seas

After mastering the winds of self-awareness and the sails of self-management, we're now ready to navigate the intricate waters of Social Awareness. This quadrant of emotional intelligence is about being attuned to others' emotions, understanding their perspectives, and recognizing the dynamics of social environments. It's like being a discerning host at a gathering, intuitively sensing the mood of your guests, making them feel understood and comfortable.

Why Social Awareness Matters

Social Awareness is essential because it facilitates stronger, more empathetic relationships. It enables you to:

Communicate more effectively: By understanding others' emotional states, you can tailor your communication to be more compassionate and effective.

Build better relationships: Empathy, a core component of social awareness, helps you connect with others on a deeper level.

Navigate social situations: Awareness of social cues and dynamics allows you to respond appropriately in various contexts, from the boardroom to the family dinner table.

A Game of Perception

Drawing from personal experience, I recall a situation where social awareness made a significant difference. During a family reunion, I noticed my uncle seemed more withdrawn than usual. Recognizing this subtle change in his demeanor, I approached him privately to offer a listening ear. It turned out he was dealing with some health issues he hadn't felt comfortable sharing with the wider family. Our conversation not only provided him with some relief but also strengthened our bond. This instance highlighted how social awareness—the ability to read and respond to others' emotions—can be a powerful tool in supporting and connecting with those around us.

Enhancing Your Social Awareness

To develop your social awareness, consider these strategies:

Practice Active Listening: Focus fully on the speaker, observing their body language and listening to their words without planning your response. This attentiveness can provide deep insights into their emotional state.

Observe Non-Verbal Cues: Much of communication is non-verbal. Pay attention to body language, facial expressions, and tone of voice to gain a fuller understanding of others' emotions and intentions.

Cultivate Empathy: Try to put yourself in others' shoes, imagining how they might feel in their situation. This empathetic perspective can significantly enhance your interactions.

Social Awareness Exercises

To strengthen your social awareness, engage in the following activities. These will help you attune to others' emotions and navigate social situations more adeptly.

Active Listening Practice: In your next conversation, concentrate on listening more than speaking. Afterward, reflect on what you learned about the other person's emotional state and perspectives.

People-Watching with Purpose: Spend some time in a public place, like a park or café, and observe the people around you. Try to infer their emotions and relationships based on non-verbal cues. This exercise can sharpen your ability to read social cues.

Empathy Expansion: Think of someone in your life who is going through a challenging time. Write a letter to them (whether or not you send it) expressing understanding and support from their perspective. This is a powerful exercise to help train your subconscious mind to let go of some of the experiences of your past that are blocking you from true emotional stability in your present and future.

Reflecting on Social Tides

As you enhance your social awareness, you'll find yourself more adept at understanding and navigating the complexities of human emotions and social interactions. This skill enriches your relationships and fosters a sense of connection and empathy with those around you.

In our journey through the emotional intelligence quadrants, the next chapter will guide us to the realm of Relationship Management, where we'll explore how to apply our understanding of emotions—both our own and others'—to build stronger, more positive connections.

Chapter 5: The Quadrant of Relationship Management

Crafting Strong Connections

Having navigated the seas of self-awareness, self-management, and social awareness, we arrive at the shores of Relationship Management. This final quadrant of emotional intelligence is about using your understanding of your own emotions and those of others to manage interactions successfully. Think of it as being the coach of a sports team, where success hinges not just on your strategy but on your ability to motivate, inspire, and manage the relationships between team members.

The Value of Relationship Management

Effective relationship management is crucial because it:

<u>*Fosters healthy, supportive relationships*</u>: By managing emotions intelligently, you can build trust and rapport, laying the foundation for strong, lasting connections.

<u>*Enhances teamwork and collaboration*</u>: Emotional intelligence helps resolve conflicts and encourages a cooperative, positive working environment.

<u>*Improves leadership skills*</u>: Leaders with high emotional intelligence can inspire and motivate their teams, driving better performance and job satisfaction.

Lessons from the Field

Reflecting on my role as a counselor and a father, I've learned that managing relationships within a family requires a delicate balance of empathy, communication, and conflict resolution. A memorable example was navigating a disagreement between my daughter and my wife regarding dessert after dinner (such a fun time, am I right?). By acknowledging each of their feelings, facilitating a calm discussion, and guiding them towards a compromise, we not only resolved the conflict but also strengthened their relationship.

This experience highlighted how effective relationship management can transform potential discord into harmony and mutual respect. Again, this is something that does take practice because these situations aren't always handled in healthy ways and sometimes things get out of control. Don't give up on the journey!

Strategies for Enhancing Relationship Management

To improve your ability in managing relationships, consider the following approaches:

Communicate Effectively: Use clear, empathetic communication to express your thoughts and feelings, and actively listen to others. This open dialogue builds understanding and trust.

Manage Conflicts Constructively: View conflicts as opportunities for growth. Approach disagreements with a calm, open mindset, seeking solutions that benefit all parties involved.

Inspire and Motivate: Whether in a leadership role or as part of a team, use your emotional intelligence to encourage and support others, helping them reach their full potential.

Relationship Management Exercises

To develop your relationship management skills, try the following exercises. These practices will help you apply emotional intelligence to strengthen your connections with others.

Feedback Exchange: With a friend or colleague, practice giving and receiving constructive feedback. Focus on expressing your thoughts and feelings clearly and listening to their response with an open mind.

Conflict Resolution Role-Play: With a partner, role-play a situation where you have differing opinions. Practice navigating conflict using empathetic communication and seeking a mutually beneficial resolution.

Gratitude Journaling: Each day, write down three things you appreciate about someone in your life. Consider sharing this with them, as expressing gratitude can significantly strengthen your relationship.

Navigating Relationships with EI

As you integrate these practices into your life, you'll find that managing relationships becomes less about navigating rough waters and more about sailing smoothly towards shared goals and deeper connections. Relationship management, underpinned by the other quadrants of emotional intelligence, is the key to enriching your interactions and fostering a supportive, understanding environment whether at home, work, or in social settings.

We've now explored all four quadrants of emotional intelligence, equipping you with the knowledge and skills to enhance your emotional intelligence journey. Remember, emotional intelligence is a continuous path of growth and learning. As you apply these principles in your daily life, you'll unlock deeper understanding, stronger relationships, and greater personal and professional fulfillment.

Chapter 6: Emotional Intelligence in Relationships

Nurturing Connections with EI

Diving deeper into the realm of emotional intelligence, it's crucial to explore its profound impact on relationships. Mastering emotional intelligence enables us to nurture connections that are rich, fulfilling, and resilient. Like a team that communicates seamlessly on the field, relationships strengthened by emotional intelligence are marked by understanding, empathy, and mutual support.

The Foundation of Secure Relationships

Julie Mennano, in her insightful book "Secure Love," emphasizes the importance of emotional safety in relationships. She argues that emotional intelligence provides the tools to create this safety, allowing individuals to express their feelings without fear of judgment or rejection. The book also highlights the concept of Attachment Theory, which gives insights to why we behave the way we do in relationships.

By recognizing and validating our partner's emotions, we lay the groundwork for a secure, loving relationship. Mennano's concept aligns with the EI quadrant of Social Awareness, highlighting the need to attune to our partner's emotional state and respond with empathy and understanding.

Expressing Love Effectively

Gary Chapman's "The Five Love Languages" offers a complementary perspective, illustrating how emotional intelligence can enhance the way we express love. Chapman identifies five primary love languages: Words of Affirmation, Acts of

Service, Receiving Gifts, Quality Time, and Physical Touch.

Understanding and speaking our partner's love language requires a high level of self-awareness and social awareness—key components of emotional intelligence. By doing so, we ensure our gestures of love are both meaningful and appreciated, strengthening the emotional bond between partners.

A Real-Life Tale of Emotional Intelligence at Play

Consider the story of Mark and Alex, a couple who struggled with communication issues. Mark valued acts of service and often expressed his love by doing things around the house or running errands for Alex. However, Alex's primary love language was words of affirmation, and she longed for verbal expressions of love and appreciation.

Becoming an E.I. Guy

Through applying the principles of emotional intelligence, particularly self-awareness and social awareness, Mark recognized this discrepancy. He began making a conscious effort to express his love through compliments and verbal affirmations. This shift had a profound impact on their relationship, increasing their emotional connection and mutual satisfaction.

When thinking of my own marriage, I initially struggled with understanding the importance of learning and speaking my wife's primary love language. We ended up taking the quiz together and I realized that her primary language is Acts of Service. One important note to take here, fellas, is that oftentimes our significant other will reveal their primary love language by requesting it in various ways. In relationships we tend to blame our partner for nagging or complaining about things constantly; in those cases, I'd say pay attention to those complaints and their love language will reveal itself pretty plainly!

Questions to Consider

How well do you understand your partner's emotional needs and love language?

In what ways can you improve your emotional responsiveness to strengthen your relationship?

Have you experienced a situation where emotional intelligence helped resolve a conflict or deepen a connection in your relationship?

<u>Check out the exercise at the end of the book to take the Love Languages quiz and complete the prompts there</u>!

Cultivating Emotional Intelligence in Relationships

As we've seen through the insights of Mennano and Chapman, and the real-life example of Mark and Alex, emotional intelligence is a powerful tool in nurturing and strengthening relationships. By fostering an environment of emotional safety, understanding our partner's unique needs, and expressing love in meaningful ways, we can create lasting, loving connections.

In the journey of emotional intelligence, relationships offer a rich field for growth and learning. By applying the principles of EI in our interactions, we not only enrich our connections but also embark on a path of personal development and fulfillment.

Chapter 7: Emotional Intelligence at Work

Elevating Professional Environments with EI

In the professional realm, emotional intelligence transforms workplaces into environments where creativity, productivity, and collaboration flourish. Like a coach fine-tuning team dynamics to achieve peak performance, emotional intelligence in the workplace facilitates understanding, resolves conflicts, and fosters an atmosphere of mutual respect and support. Being able to have this wisdom of EI to put the right players into the proper position, you put the team in a great space to be successful. It's also important to know that even though you may put them in the best position, it does not mean they will flawlessly execute the game plan. Having emotional intelligence to coach a player through their mistakes can make a huge difference!

Cultivating High Performance and Leadership

In "The 5AM Club," Robin Sharma discusses the importance of personal mastery and leadership, both of which are deeply connected to emotional intelligence. Sharma suggests that rising early contributes to greater personal discipline, clarity of thought, and emotional well-being, which are essential components of emotional intelligence. Leaders who practice these principles set a powerful example for their teams, promoting a culture of high performance and emotional resilience. Emotional intelligence, in this context, enhances a leader's ability to connect with their team, inspire motivation, and navigate the challenges of leadership with empathy and strategic insight.

Additionally, those that are not yet in leadership roles, these principles can apply to better increase your value within an organization and heighten your chances for upward mobility. These skills are intangible, meaning that they can translate across all different types of teams and organizations.

The Power of Rethinking and Flexibility

Adam Grant's "Think Again" underscores the value of rethinking and mental flexibility, crucial aspects of the self-management and relationship management quadrants of emotional intelligence. Grant advocates for the importance of being open to changing one's mind and encourages cultivating a culture of learning and psychological safety in the workplace. This approach requires a high degree of emotional intelligence, particularly in recognizing and managing one's own emotional reactions to new ideas and in fostering an environment where others feel safe to express dissenting opinions and challenge the status quo. By leading by example, others can feel encouraged to explore the importance of these skills, as well.

A Real-Life Example of EI in Action

Consider the story of Sarah, a project manager who led a diverse team facing a tight deadline on a high-stakes project. Tensions and stress levels were high, with frequent conflicts arising between team members. Drawing on her emotional intelligence, Sarah recognized the emotional undercurrents fueling these tensions. She organized a series of team meetings focused on open communication, where team members were encouraged to express their concerns and frustrations in a constructive manner. Sarah listened empathetically, validated her team's feelings, and worked with them to find mutually agreeable solutions to workflow bottlenecks.

By applying EI principles, she not only defused the tension but also fostered a stronger, more cohesive team dynamic that successfully met the project deadline. See what emotional consistency can give you?

Questions to Consider

How can you apply emotional intelligence to improve communication and collaboration within your team?

What role does emotional intelligence play in leadership and influencing workplace culture?

Can you recall a situation where emotional intelligence helped you or a colleague navigate a challenging workplace scenario?

Conclusion: Integrating EI for Workplace Excellence

As illustrated through the insights from "The 5AM Club" and "Think Again," along with the real-life example of Sarah's project team, emotional intelligence is a key driver of professional success and satisfaction. Whether in leadership positions or general staff roles, cultivating emotional intelligence can significantly enhance workplace dynamics, performance, and overall well-being. By committing to the continuous development of our emotional intelligence, we empower ourselves and others to thrive in today's fast-paced, ever-changing professional landscapes.

Chapter 8: Emotional Intelligence as a Father

Fostering Emotional Growth in the Family

Emotional intelligence (EI) plays a pivotal role in parenting, especially in the context of fatherhood. It empowers fathers to nurture their children's emotional development, build strong family bonds, and navigate the complexities of parenting with empathy and understanding. Additionally, it is important to ensure our emotional intelligence skills are on point in order to remain on the same page with the other parent as consistently as possible. Like a gardener tending to different plants, a father uses emotional intelligence to provide the specific care and support each child needs to thrive.

Mindful Parenting with Emotional Intelligence

In "Raising Good Humans," Hunter Clarke-Fields emphasizes the importance of mindfulness and emotional regulation in parenting. Clarke-Fields argues that a parent's ability to manage their own emotions directly influences their interactions with their children and teaches them, by example, how to handle their own feelings. This aspect of emotional intelligence is crucial for fathers who strive to respond to their children's needs with patience and empathy, rather than reacting out of frustration or anger. I know we can all recall a time when we were met by a parent or caregiver who did not show the patience and compassion that we probably needed in that moment. Try to be thoughtful of this when you find yourself becoming impatient.

Understanding Your Child's Emotional Love Language

Gary Chapman's "The Five Love Languages of Children" extends the concept of love languages to the parent-child relationship, highlighting how emotional intelligence can guide fathers in understanding and meeting their children's emotional and love needs. Chapman posits that each child expresses and receives love in one of five ways: Words of Affirmation, Acts of Service, Receiving Gifts, Quality Time, or Physical Touch. Recognizing and speaking your child's primary love language fosters a deeper emotional connection and a sense of security and belonging.

A Real-Life Illustration of EI in Fatherhood

Consider the story of David, a father who noticed his daughter, Mia, becoming increasingly withdrawn and moody. Drawing on his emotional intelligence, David recognized that scolding Mia for her attitude would likely exacerbate the situation. Instead, he chose to spend quality time with her, engaging in activities she enjoyed and gently opening the door to conversation. Over time, Mia opened up about struggling with bullying at school.

Understanding her love language was quality time; David's decision to actively spend time with her created a safe space for Mia to express her feelings and for David to provide the support and guidance she needed.

I think it's important to note that for the most part, children are going to truly show you that they feel loved in all these languages fluently early on. My daughters, six and three years old, are very receptive of all these languages at certain times. The key is to be strategic and understand which language your babies are seeking at the right moment. Pay attention to the questions they ask!

Questions to Consider

How well do you understand the emotional needs and love languages of your children?

Reflect on a recent parenting challenge. How could emotional intelligence have influenced the outcome?

In what ways can you model emotional intelligence for your children?

<u>Observation</u>: Spend a week observing your child's emotional expressions, reactions, and preferences. Take notes on what seems to make them feel loved, happy, anxious, or upset.

<u>Engagement</u>: Based on your observations, intentionally engage with your child using their primary love language. For example, if their love language is Words of Affirmation, make an extra effort to verbally express your love and appreciation for them.

Reflection: At the end of the week, reflect on any changes in your child's behavior or in your relationship with them. Discuss your observations with your child, asking for their feedback on how they felt during the week.

Nurturing Emotional Intelligence in Fatherhood

Drawing insights from "Raising Good Humans" and "The Five Love Languages of Children," along with David and Mia's story, it's clear that emotional intelligence is a vital tool in the journey of fatherhood. It enables fathers to connect with their children on a deeper level, understand their unique emotional needs, and guide them through life's challenges with empathy and wisdom. By committing to developing their emotional intelligence, fathers can build strong, resilient families where every member feels understood, valued, and loved.

Conclusion

The Transformative Power of Emotional Intelligence

As we conclude our journey, it's important to reflect on the transformative power of emotional intelligence (EI) across the diverse landscapes of our lives. From enhancing personal growth and fostering meaningful relationships to elevating our professional lives and enriching our roles as fathers, EI serves as a guiding light, illuminating the path to a more fulfilled and balanced existence.

A Journey of Continuous Growth

Emotional intelligence is not a destination but a continuous journey of growth and self-discovery. Like a gardener who nurtures their garden through the seasons, tending to it with care and attention, we must nurture our emotional intelligence with patience, practice, and persistence. The seeds we've planted together—self-awareness, self-management, social awareness, and relationship management—require ongoing cultivation to thrive.

The Ripple Effect of Emotional Intelligence

The development of our emotional intelligence creates a ripple effect, touching every aspect of our lives and the lives of those around us. By managing our emotions effectively, we not only improve our own well-being but also contribute to a more compassionate, understanding, and emotionally healthy world. As we become more emotionally intelligent, we inspire those around us to embark on their own journeys of emotional growth.

Becoming an E.I. Guy

Let this book be your starter guide—a challenge to elevate your emotional intelligence and, with it, your life. Remember, the journey does not end here. Every day presents new opportunities to apply and expand your emotional intelligence. Whether you're navigating the complexities of relationships, striving for excellence in you+--r professional life, or fostering a loving environment for your family, emotional intelligence is your steadfast ally. It'll be a superpower that you never knew that you had, but you will reap the benefits within the first month of using it!

Moving Forward with Purpose and Passion

As we part ways, I encourage you to move forward with purpose and passion, using the insights and strategies from this book as a compass. Embrace the challenges and opportunities that come your way, viewing them through the lens of emotional intelligence. Continue to learn, grow, and evolve, and remember that the journey to becoming an emotionally intelligent man is one of the most rewarding journeys you can undertake.

In the words of Gary Chapman and Hunter Clarke-Fields, understanding and speaking the love languages of those around us, whether they be partners, children, or colleagues, can transform our interactions and deepen our connections. Let us carry these lessons forward, weaving emotional intelligence into the fabric of our daily lives, and watch as the world around us transforms in response.

Thank you for embarking on this journey with me. May the path ahead be enriched with growth, understanding, and emotional fulfillment. Here's to the newer, emotionally intelligent you. Peace!!!

This page was intentionally left blank

Becoming an E.I. Guy

HOW TO USE THIS WORKBOOK

Daily Emotional Journal Exercise and Weekly Check-In:

This is a daily guide to assist you with keeping track of your emotions; the first quadrant of Emotional Intelligence. Use the 'Emotion Wheel' to practice identifying emotions we often ignore or disregard.

At the end of each week, use the Weekly Check-In to gauge your progress.

Emotional Self-Awareness Reflection:

After 4 weeks, look at these questions and answer them truthfully.

The worksheets for *EI in Relationships*, *EI in the Workplace*, and *EI as a Father* are to be completed either concurrently while you are reading the book, or following the 28 days upon completion.

Daily Emotion Journaling Exercise:

For the next 28 days, write down at least one significant emotional experience you have each day, using the Emotion Wheel on the next page.

Note what triggered the emotion, how you reacted, and what outcome your reaction led to.

Reflect on how understanding your emotional response better could have changed the outcome.

Day	Emotion	Trigger	Outcome	Diff Outcome?
1				
2				
3				
4				
5				
6				

Becoming an E.I. Guy

7				
8				
9				
10				
11				
12				
13				
14				
15				
16				
17				
18				
19				

Becoming an E.I. Guy

20				
21				
22				
23				
24				
25				
26				
27				
28				

Becoming an E.I. Guy

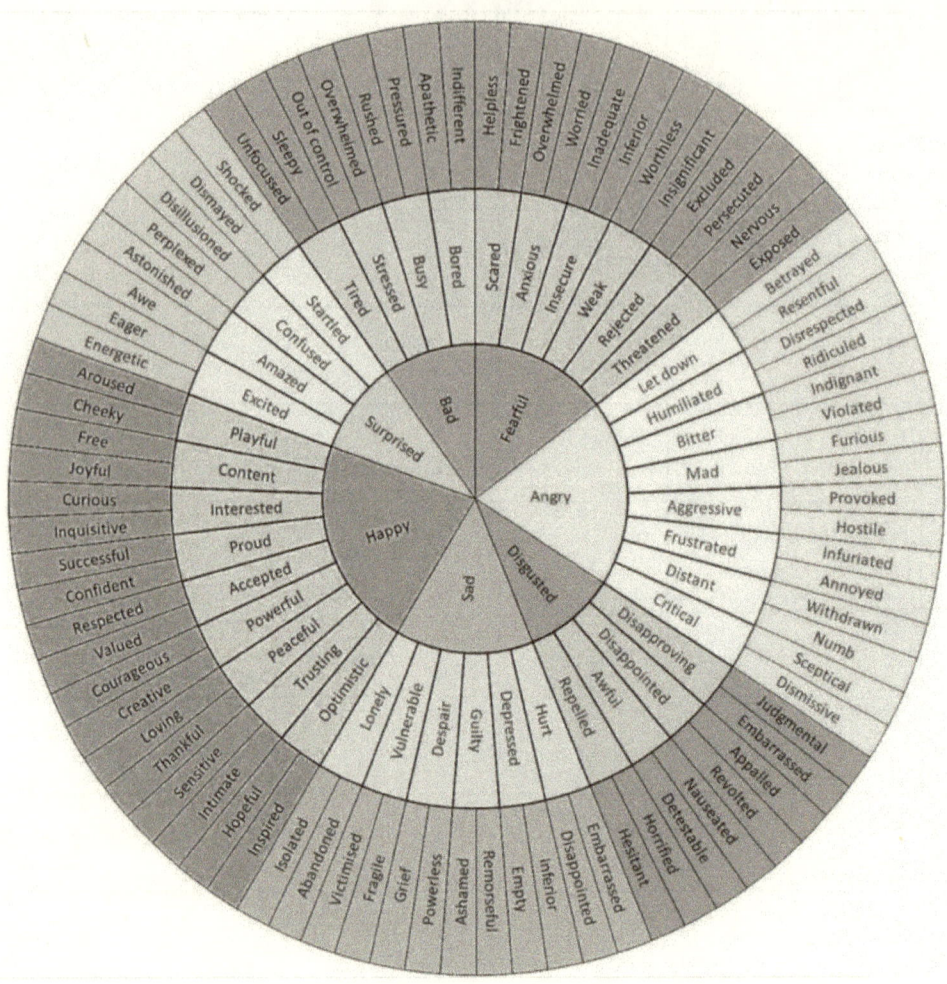

Emotional Self-Awareness Reflection

At the end of the month, answer the following questions based on your patterns:

What were the predominant emotions I felt?

_____
_____
_____
_____
_____
_____
_____
_____

What triggered these emotions?

_____
_____
_____
_____

_____
_____
_____
_____

How did I react to these emotions? Was it effective?

_____
_____
_____
_____
_____
_____
_____

How did my emotions affect my interactions with others?

_____
_____

Becoming an E.I. Guy

_____
_____
_____
_____
_____
_____
_____
_____

What did I learn from this month's emotional experiences?

_____
_____
_____
_____
_____

Becoming an E.I. Guy

_____
_____
_____
_____
_____
_____

Emotional Intelligence in Relationships

Discover your and your partner's primary love languages through discussion or taking the love languages quiz at https://5lovelanguages.com/quizzes/love-language

Your Primary Language:
_____

Your Partner's Language:
_____

Apply this knowledge by expressing love in your partner's primary love language daily for a week. What did you learn?

_____
_____
_____
_____
_____
_____

Becoming an E.I. Guy

Reflect on any changes in the emotional climate of your relationship.

_____
_____
_____
_____
_____

Becoming an E.I. Guy

Emotional Intelligence in the Workplace

Reflect on a recent work-related challenge, focusing on the emotional aspects.

_____
_____
_____
_____
_____
_____
_____
_____
_____
_____
_____

Develop an action plan to enhance one aspect of your emotional intelligence in the workplace.

Becoming an E.I. Guy

Implement your plan over the next month, journaling your experiences and progress.

Becoming an E.I. Guy

Emotional Intelligence as a Father

Emotional Awareness Week with Your Child:

Spend a week observing your child's emotional expressions and reactions.

Engage with your child using their primary love language, noting any changes in behavior or your relationship.

Reflect on the exercise with your child, discussing how it felt and what you both learned.

_____
_____
_____
_____
_____
_____
_____
_____
_____
_____

Becoming an E.I. Guy

Becoming an E.I. Guy

Weekly Check-in

At the end of each week, reflect on your progress with the exercises.

	Challenges Faced	How did you overcome?	Insights Gained This Week
Week 1			
Week 2			
Week 3			
Week 4			

Emotional Intelligence Check-In

At the end of each month, assess your growth in each EI quadrant.

	Areas of Strength	**Areas for Development**
Self-Awareness		
Self-Management		
Social Awareness		
Relationship Management		

Becoming an E.I. Guy

Goal Setting and Tracking

Going forward, set some SMART long-term goals for your Emotional Intelligence (SMART) Track your progress towards these goals.

Specific – What *specifically* is your goal as it relates to Emotional Intelligence?	
Measurable – How will you measure this progress?	
Achievable – How do you plan to achieve this goal?	
Relevant – Why is your goal relevant to your life?	
Time-Bound – How long will this goal take to achieve? When are you going to start?	

ABOUT THE AUTHOR

Evan Hunter Jr. (EJ) was born and raised in Waterbury, Connecticut. He is a graduate of Western Connecticut State University (Bachelor – Justice Law Administration) and a postgraduate of Post University (Counseling). He is a licensed professional counselor and licensed alcohol and drug counselor in Connecticut and is also a member of Phi Beta Sigma Fraternity, Incorporated.

Becoming an E.I. Guy

© 2024 Evan Hunter Jr., LPC, LADC. All rights reserved.

Published by Forward Progress Counseling LLC.

No part of this publication may be reproduced, distributed, or transmitted in any form or by any means, including photocopying, recording, or other electronic or mechanical methods, without the prior written permission of the publisher, except in the case of brief quotations embodied in critical reviews and certain other noncommercial uses permitted by copyright law. For permission requests, write to the publisher, addressed "Attention: Permissions Coordinator," at

ejhunter@fowardprogresscounseling.org.

www.ingramcontent.com/pod-product-compliance
Lightning Source LLC
Chambersburg PA
CBHW031125160426
43192CB00008B/1115